Perels of Wisdom

Tapping into the Peace Within

Todd Perelmuter

Perels of Wisdom

DEDICATION

I dedicate this book to all living beings, for if even a single being didn't exist exactly as they are, this book would not have been possible. This is no exaggeration, for we are all deeply connected in ways both seen and unseen. With the deepest of love and gratitude, I thank you.

CONTENTS

1.

You are not your thoughts.
You are not your past.
You are not your failings.
You are not your suffering.
You are not the story you tell yourself about your life.
These are simply thought forms. They are fleeting objects that only exist in the mind. They are temporary sense perceptions recalled by the mind, remembering very brief moments from the past that in actuality make up a very small percentage of your entire life.

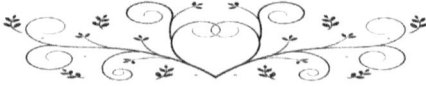

2.

Every moment is a choice. The more we do the right thing even when it's hard, the more we are creating the habit to face adversity when it comes into our lives head-on with grace and elegance and peace and calm. We are training our minds to embrace difficulty so that whatever comes at us in our lives, we are prepared for it and it will not disrupt our inner peace because we've trained for this and we can overcome anything.

3.

Every action we take is done out of a search for happiness. And yet, all we find is momentary pleasure followed by more craving and more longing. We seek out pleasure and try to avoid pain, but no matter how well we do, we don't find lasting happiness. Don't expect to find happiness in anything because that's not true happiness. That is only momentary pleasure dependent on specific external factors, often followed by pain. For true lasting happiness, we have to discover that deep peace that we can only find by looking inward, in the stillness, in the space, and not in the stuff so much.

4.

We cannot grow without pain, and by going through pain and surviving, we become examples to the world that they're not alone, that they can overcome their pain as well, and that they can do better and get better.

5.

It's not easy to meditate when you've spent decades constantly thinking, constantly doing, constantly being entertained, and constantly buried in work or pleasure. But that is why we must use this moment right here, right now, to undo that habit of compulsively looking for what's next, seeking pleasure, and avoiding pain. And start training our minds to be present and at peace in everything we do.

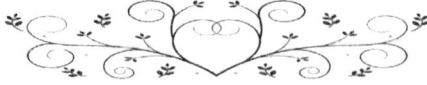

6.

In the present moment, there is only experience itself — no labels, judgments, opinions or criticisms. Just bliss and oneness between you and what you are witnessing because you realize that all experience happens within.

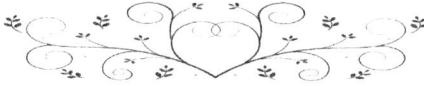

7.

A hug or a hand on someone else's is the simplest but most profound act of showing love and compassion. It can instantly transform our mental and emotional states. In just one instant, it communicates to someone that they are not alone and that someone is there for them. So, don't be afraid to use the power of touch to heal someone.

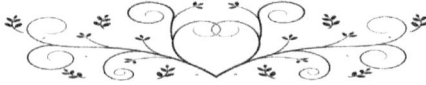

8.

There is awe and wonder and beauty in everything. If you don't see it, you have to just look deeper because it's there. To the blind, the sound is a miracle. To the deaf, color is magic. No matter who or where you are, there is magic and incredible beauty to discover in every moment, and looking for it is a joy.

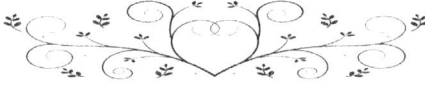

9.

The key to living fully in the now and letting go of the past is really the practice of meditation — observing each present breath and just observing whatever arises in your field of consciousness. Make a habit of keeping your mind in the present moment and as your mind wanders, simply and gently bring it back to the present moment.

10.

When we become unconscious of what we're doing, we switch to autopilot, stop being fully present, and become completely unaware of the subtleties and nuances that make each moment different. Even though everything is new, vibrant, exciting, and different, we create this mental projection that it's the same, that it's boring. And this makes us feel stuck in life.

11.

If the desire to change is coming from a place of growth, it's fantastic. But if it's coming from a place of boredom and impatience, then it's time to practice mindfulness to find that newness again.

12.

Ultimately, oneness is the realization that we can never truly be alone.

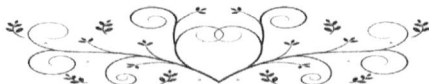

13.

The words "aloneness" and "loneliness" are very similar but in meaning, they are miles apart. Loneliness is suffering from being alone. Aloneness contains the word oneness in it and it really is all about recognizing the interconnectedness of all things, sensing the oneness but not feeling lonely. There's no negativity, no suffering, just oneness with everyone and everything.

14.

The key to self-worth isn't in getting to be the most attractive person or have the most followers on social media. Striving for some idealized version of oneself based on today's fleeting trends can itself create insecurity and feelings of worthlessness. Social media only makes the problem worse with its filters and endless content. The key to self-worth is inner strength and inner peace.

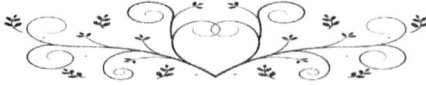

15.

You are not your body, because the cells in your body are not the same cells as when you were born. You are not your thoughts, because they are constantly changing. You are also not your memories, which fade. Nor are you your made-up sense of identity, i.e. sister, mother, doctor, husband, etc... You are a point of consciousness.

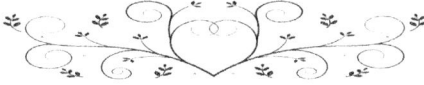

16.

The more conscious of our time we become, the more we start doing things that make us joyful instead of making us miserable - spending more time with friends and family and appreciating ourselves and others for the kind of character that they have.

17.

Every single person deserves to be treated with love, respect and dignity. Toxic situations and toxic people have no place in your life.
You don't have to sacrifice your peace for someone else.
You don't have to put yourself in a position to be taken advantage of or abused.
Sometimes, the greatest act of love is a kind and peaceful "NO."
No to cruelty.
No to trauma.
No to toxicity.

18.

Many little comments from our childhood hurt us so much and stay with us for so long. It is only together that we can really heal, that we can let go, and that we can share our troubles and our joys. Sometimes, we don't always get the support we need, but we can always give it to others, and in turn, we heal ourselves.

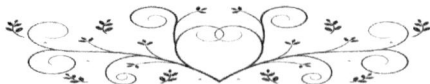

19.

By simply remembering the preciousness of each moment, to see how short our lives are and how valuable each moment is, we can face the unknown and we can conquer our fear. We can become more present, more joyful, and have a greater zest for life with no fear — only excitement for the great unknown.

20.

Everything we do is a projection of what we're thinking and feeling. The human mind cannot understand the difference between kindness to someone else and kindness to yourself, between loving yourself or loving someone else, criticizing yourself or criticizing someone else, because the feeling is the same. If you hate, there is hate in your heart. If you love, the world becomes loving.

21.

Just because you can't see in the moment how a kind act reverberates out into the world like a ripple in a lake, spreading out in infinite ways in every direction, doesn't mean that it didn't happen. Every action creates a reaction. That act of kindness has a cause and effect. Even if the effect seems unnoticeable, it is there.

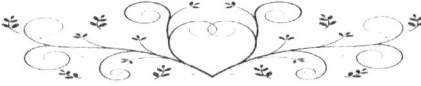

22.

Only through meditation and mindfulness can we truly see things from the broadest perspective possible. We don't make ourselves the victim because we don't frame circumstances as happening to us. We don't compare our possessions with someone else who has more. Instead, we simply watch the play of life unfold. This is the secret to living a joyful, peaceful life.

23.

What daily little inconvenience or annoyance, traffic or bad boss can hold a candle to the infinite, eternal awesomeness of the universe? So, whenever we get bogged down in the day-to-day issues and difficulties, all we have to do is remember, think about, and focus on this incredible miracle of existence.

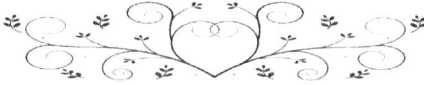

24.

When we set intentions for gratitude, love, kindness and generosity, and as we practice these traits, we are planting positive seeds and tending to our mind-garden so beautiful things can grow. The more we engage in gossip and mindlessly consume news or social media, the more we're planting seeds of envy, hatred, fear and unhappiness.

25.

Many of us may know people who have buried their heads in work for so long and for so much of their lives. They escape into their work to avoid any unpleasant feelings. They resist healing themselves by diving deeper into their work. Society often rewards this. Many of these people can't even retire because this is the only way they've learned to deal with painful emotions. All because being with themselves and their thoughts is too unbearable.

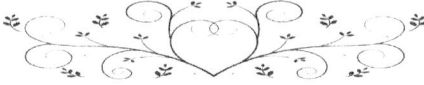

26.

With mindfulness, we can even thank our exes for showing us their true colors, and for letting us know sooner rather than later that the relationship wasn't right. We can move on and find that special someone we were meant for. It may take a while, but the more you put yourself out there, the sooner it'll happen. You just have to be courageous, be present, be open, and know deep down that you'll be happy, you'll be at peace, and you'll be grateful with whatever may come and go in life.

27.

This is your world. Do you want to live in a world of more kindness or less kindness? So be kind, even when no one's looking, and you will live in a more kind world. As we never know what other people are going through, sometimes all they need is kindness.

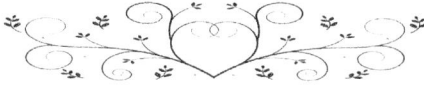

28.

We all have these self-constructed personalities and we believe that our likes and dislikes make up a strong part of our personality and who we are. But, we can choose our own likes and dislikes. They don't have to just be automatic unconscious reactions.

29.

Self-loathing is a terrible affliction born out of the false perception that we are our thoughts. It divides each of us into two people rather than being one whole complete person. This illusion falsely implies you can love or hate yourself, but in reality, you can't have a relationship with yourself. You simply are you. A relationship with yourself can only happen if you believe you are split in two. By recognizing your one true self, all self-loathing ceases to be.

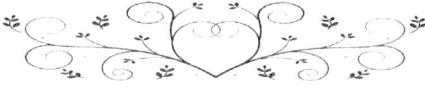

30.

When we are aware of our own infinite reservoir of peace, love and joy, we no longer make unhealthy choices, we don't chase pleasures that'll make us feel good now but feel sick later because we're not trying to fill some spiritual hole in our heart. Instead, we make good choices that'll make us feel good later and that we can feel good about now. But when we are not aware of that love and happiness we have below all those shallow thoughts, we try to fill the emptiness because we're not aware of our fullness.

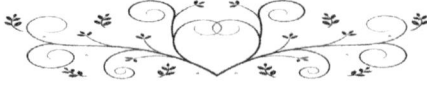

31.

God and the universe are really interchangeable words. The universe loves us, God loves us. Have faith in the universe, have faith in God. It's all the same. If God is everywhere then God is the universe and you don't have to believe in God to believe in the universe.

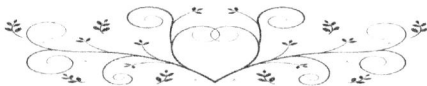

32.

So often we relive the worst moments of our lives over and over and over again. We spend so much of our lives living out our worst imagined fears of the future. When we consciously become aware of it, we realize what a horrible way it is to live.

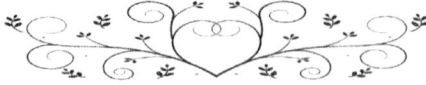

33.

The more we can sit with our thoughts and then slow our breathing, bring our breath to a calm, slow, deep pace while feeling these very disturbing emotions, we're actually bringing inner peace. The pain is still there and it sits with us, and it may be there for the rest of our lives, but we can sit with it in peace. It may take days or weeks or months or years, but the more we can sit without distraction and feel without being afraid of these feelings, not resist these feelings, just accept and make peace with them, this is how the healing happens.

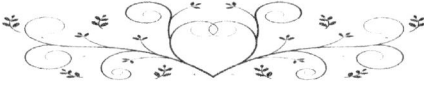

34.

In reality, our worst nightmares are not as scary as we imagined them to be and it is through challenges only that we learn, grow and evolve.

35.

Observe your thoughts without being lost in your thoughts. Just become mindful of them.

36.

There's a Buddhist meditation that anyone can do where you sit with someone else (friends, relatives, life partners) and you just stare into their eyes for an extended period of time. At first, it feels awkward and weird and you want to look away. But as you break through this discomfort, there arises a great sense of the two becoming one, ego dissolves, selfishness dissolves, and there remains a powerful connection that is truly healing and transformative in ways that sometimes meditating alone can never do.

37.

I once met a 96-year-old woman so full of life she didn't seem over 55. She was a fishing boat captain her whole life. She retired at around 70 and wasn't sure what to do with her time. So, she started to write even though she had never written before. When I met her, she was reading an excerpt from her eighth novel, her eighth best-selling novel. I'll keep this woman's example with me for the rest of my life because she is the definition of what it means to never be too old to start over, it's never too late to try something new.

38.

Welcome the unknown, accept uncertainty and try not to respond with doubt and worry. Trust that each moment will happen as it will and in the end everything will work out. Just allow this moment to be.

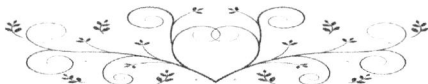

39.

We're never too old and it's never too late to try something we've not done before. As you start a new adventure, inexperienced and wide-eyed, as you see your progress over time, your skills improving and your new life blossoming, you'll know the journey was worth taking.

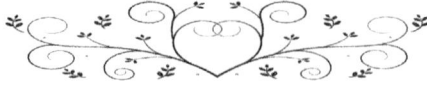

40.

Don't be afraid to be generous. When your act of generosity is returned, you will know that these are your people, these are the kind ones. And soon, your life will overflow with beautiful, generous souls. Some people may not respond with generosity, but the worst that can happen is you discover who aren't your people sooner rather than later, and it will save you in headaches and in more costly ways down the road.

41.

In our normal mode of thinking, we may say our neighbor has more money than us. In our higher consciousness, we appreciate whatever we have. In our normal mode of thinking,

We compare our looks to those around us — in the billboards, the magazines, the movies, etc... In mindfulness, we appreciate life itself and our inner wisdom, our heart, our intuition. We see and appreciate that same beauty and nature in others. We don't compare. There's no jealousy. We simply see and appreciate the beauty all around us and within.

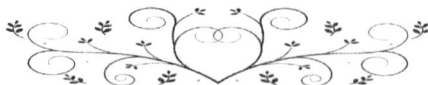

42.

Our lives are no more important than ants, and yet, no less important than anyone else's. It is quite simply a miracle, this dance of life, is playing out in all its beauty exactly as it's supposed to. Our insignificance is significant, but the meaning we create in our lives is limitless.

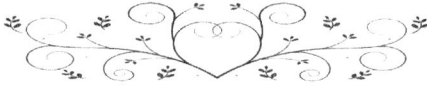

43.

Everything we do stems from the quality of our minds. Our mindset dictates our thoughts, our thoughts dictate our words, our words dictate our actions, and our actions turn into habits.

44.

The more we can be happy for other people's successes and happy with our own shortcomings, the happier we will be.

45.

Fear is the worst part of any life change, because when the change actually comes, once we make peace with it and accept it, we can handle it. We simply have to relax, meditate, and put our awareness into our body where our stressful breathing is happening and anywhere else we're holding on to tension in our body. Only then can we release it, get comfortable, and really sit deeply and sink into the peace that is always there, with no resistance.

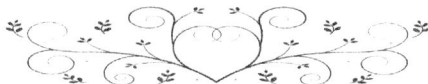

46.

The more we practice expressing gratitude and love, the more things we will find to be grateful for and the more love we'll have in our lives. The more we practice just being present and getting outside of our heads, the clearer we can see our situations, the greater wisdom we will have and the greater awareness we will have of our own thoughts. Through this heightened awareness comes a peacefulness because our thoughts no longer dictate our experience. They just become another observation within our field of perception.

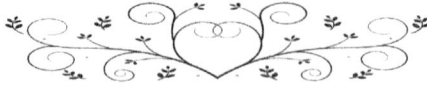

47.

Breaking up with someone can be as difficult as a loved one passing away. This is because we're not just dealing with loss, but also feelings of rejection, issues with self-worth, and even blaming ourselves. It is in these times that having the skills to sit in solitude and to find peace in the present moment are more important than ever. These are the times to show ourselves extra love and compassion, to look inward, to heal and to process, and there's no greater way to do that than through the transformative and simple practice of meditation.

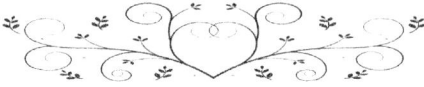

48.

Anxiety and stress are like waves washing on shore to the beach. If you ignore the waves, they'll still be there. And, as hard as you may try to stop the waves from coming on shore, they'll still come ashore. Both ignoring them, and forcing them to stop, won't work — just like stress and anxiety. But, if you start to pay attention to the infinitely deep, calm water underneath the surface, then it will shift your perspective and you will suddenly realize that these seemingly turbulent waves are so small compared to the joy and love and depth in our lives. We only need to become familiar with the peace beneath the waves.

49.

Everything we do can be a meditative practice if we use it as an opportunity to practice being present in the moment. Walking can be a meditation. Eating can be a meditation. Each is a profound experience that can become even more profound when we're fully present, when we feel every step, and taste every flavor.

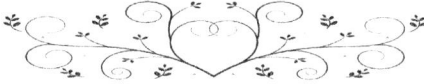

50.

Self-loathing is a terrible affliction born out of the false perception that we are our thoughts. It divides each of us into two people rather than being one whole complete person. This illusion falsely implies you can love or hate yourself, but in reality, you can't have a relationship with yourself. You simply are you. A relationship with yourself can only happen if you believe you are split in two. By recognizing your one true self, all self-loathing ceases to be.

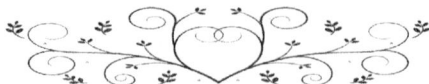

51.

The right teacher or guide will show themselves to you in your life at the right time when you need it so be aware of what happens and be open to experiences.

52.

Death is the great equalizer. No matter how rich or how poor, we're all going in the same direction.

53.

Birth and death are really illusions. There really is no beginning and there is no end. Before this life, we were alive in our parents and before that, we were alive in our grandparents and our ancestors. One thing gets passed on to another. One form changes to another.

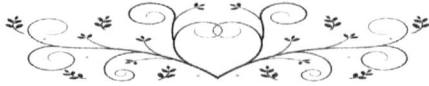

54.

If we are dealing with stress and anxiety in negative ways or ignoring them, we will continue to suffer poor health and be miserable. So, you want to practice observing your own state of mind, allowing some space to just sit with yourself, and really connecting with this deep peace that lies within all of us.

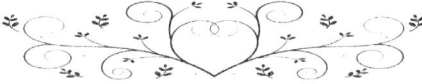

55.

When we lose a pet and that loss seems unbearable and the suffering feels too immense, it's important to allow that feeling to have its space because this is the only way we can heal and process and then eventually let go. We may want to bury ourselves in work or distract ourselves, but it's okay to feel these feelings, and resisting it will only create more emotional disturbance.

56.

When we think, we think one word at a time. When we speak, we speak one word at a time. But when we feel, when we sense, we can take in thousands and millions of sense perceptions all at once and we can tune into this understanding, this deeper wisdom. And, we can share this "beingness" with another person where we can commune with their soul and truly get a sense of their being much more effectively than in our normal mode of communication. So do not be afraid to sit with someone. Do not be afraid of silence. Do not feel the need to always fill it because simply being there for someone, just by being with them and giving their being all of your being is the most powerful healing and transformative experience we can have.

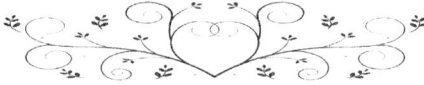

57.

When you have fear of rejection or fear of failure, then it's really important to turn inward and spend some time really looking at your fears and analyzing them. They can be coming from a place of fear - a fear of trying new things or a fear of stillness or a fear of being alone with your thoughts or fear of unknown experiences.

58.

Our senses are the doorway to the present moment and the more we expand our awareness in every moment, the less we're lost in our thoughts, and the more we're fully living and getting the most out of our lives.

59.

If you are self-aware enough to know that you want a
different job, maybe a different boss, then by all means start
job hunting. But if you're not sure, I would highly encourage
you to start a meditation practice and to use mindfulness
meditation to bring mindfulness to your job. Because stress,
anxiety, poor health — these are unconscious reactions to
our situations. And the more mindful we become of our
stress, the more it's possible to release stress and find
whatever we end up doing much more enjoyable.

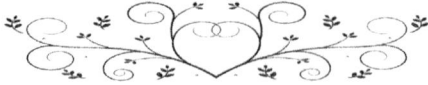

60.

There is a middle ground, a path of balance, where we can both learn from the past, plan for the future, and still fully appreciate and live in the present moment. To fully live in the present moment is to react to the present moment with full consciousness, with full wisdom, and awareness.

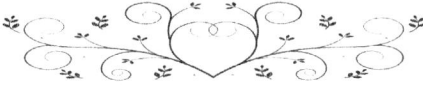

61.

There are so many different kinds of meditation and they're each incredibly valuable, and profound and have different amazing benefits. So, there's no reason to limit yourself to just one type of meditation.

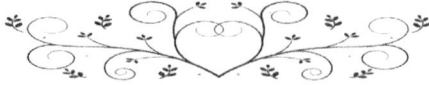

62.

In a world of attention deficit and constant distractions, it's even more valuable to just be with someone. You don't have to say the right thing. Simply spending time with someone is the most wonderful thing you can do. That's why they call it "pay" attention and "spend" time because it's investing in others and it's more priceless than any physical gift.

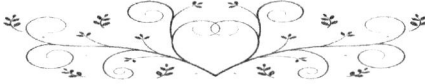

63.

Oftentimes it is the people who suffered the most who have the quickest and easiest path to enlightenment and self-actualization. This is because they've been through so much. They are survivors. They are fighters and if that is you, we need your lessons. We need your example, so share it with the world. You are the light that will lead the way out for so many people.

64.

Without struggles, there would be no striving to be better, to overcome, to acquire the skills and strength to evolve as people. These are struggles that make us beautiful. Without difficulty, without suffering, no one would be on the path to self-actualization.

65.

Every single one of us will get sick and die. Everyone we know and love will too. There's no escaping, but it is these hardest moments, these most difficult times, that show what we're truly made of and what we can truly overcome.

66.

When we become more aware of the connections and the relationships between us and all living beings, then we feel wonder and awe in everything because we see ourselves and we see oneness everywhere we look.

67.

If there was no suffering, there would be no striving for that inner joy and inner peace. There would be no wisdom gained or learning from mistakes. And the more we allow ourselves to consciously process traumatic experiences from our past, the less suffering we have in the present.

68.

We are conscious intentions of how we wish to move forward in life. And conscious intentions become conscious thoughts, which become conscious behaviors, and then conscious habits that are positive, healing, and lead to lasting inner peace and joy.

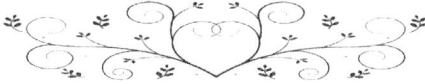

69.

We always make the choice that we think is best. Nobody is making a choice that they think is going to lead to suffering later on. We're all doing the very best with what we know at a certain time, which is always very limited information. So, when we take a step back and look at the big picture, we can see now that there's really no need to be hard on ourselves, or others, for making the wrong decision.

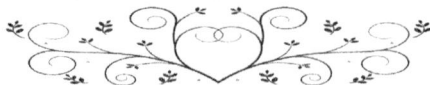

70.

The more we sit with our thoughts and really get to know ourselves, the more we understand our true calling and purpose in life. By sitting with ourselves in peace and quiet, we bring more peace into our lives and we give ourselves the space to process and heal from our emotions. The more we process our thoughts and heal, the more we can let go, forgive, leave the past, let the future be in the future, and take solace in the present moment.

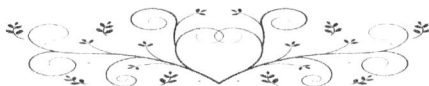

71.

Everyone is trying to be some idealized version that's mostly created by Hollywood or put out by the fashion industry and amplified by social media. But it's not healthy to be constantly inundated by all of these images and comparing ourselves to the most beautiful person on the planet. Accept yourself for who you are and be confident in who you are and that you are the miracle of life itself.

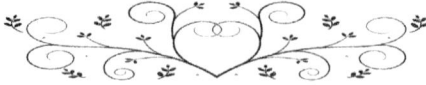

72.

As soon as you notice you're anxious, bring your mind to your thoughts without judgment or labeling. Just observe what your mind is thinking about because it's almost always unconscious thinking that is taking place, and the best thing we can do is to turn that unconscious thinking into conscious thinking.

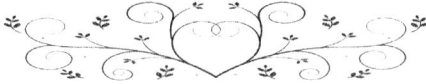

73.

When we are just in the moment, there are no doubts, there are no worries, and there's no room for anxiety.

74.

We are that light of consciousness — that which perceives. And it's the same light that's in you and me and everyone else.

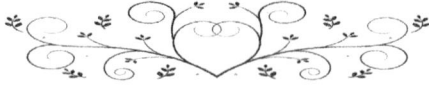

75.

We each get treated how we allow others to treat us and a peaceful "no" is more positive than a "yes" that comes from a place of just wishing to please others. Every one of us deserves relationships that respect and honor each person, not having to change our truth to make others feel better, or change our opinion to make them feel better, or bite our tongue because we feel unsafe to express ourselves.

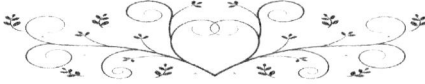

76.

It's so important to be able to be truthful and not passive-aggressive with our closest relationships because passive aggression will only lead to more trouble down the line. It is only in truth and honesty that strong relationships can be built.

77.

There is beauty in learning a new thing or taking a leap of faith and trying something new. Whether it's learning a new instrument or learning a new language, working towards something and achieving it is its own reward.

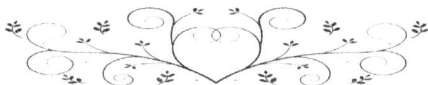

78.

Your thoughts, words and actions are incredibly powerful. They create ripple effects that can change the world. Kindness is the only way to live in the world if we wish to live in a world of kindness. We are always with ourselves, so we might as well be with a kind person.

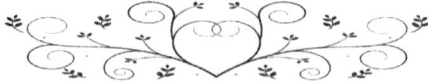

79.

Kindness is not the same as niceness. They're often mistaken for each other but they are worlds apart. Kindness comes from wisdom and compassion. It means telling someone something they need to hear in a loving way that will help them. Nice is ignoring something that may be difficult to talk about, or it may be allowing someone to continue harmful behavior just because you want to be nice and you just want to let it slide. That would not be kind to yourself, them, or the people they will hurt in the future.

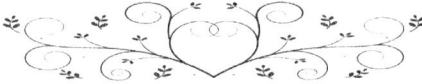

80.

Acts of kindness make us feel better. The better we feel, the more at peace we are and the more kindness we attract to ourselves. The more generous we are, the more generosity we see in others.

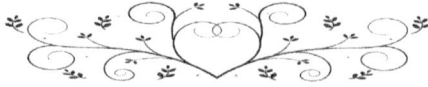

81.

In meditation, when we give ourselves the time to close our eyes and sit in stillness and quiet, we disconnect from the material world and we turn our senses inward. We're able to simply be and experience the interconnectedness of all things and beings.

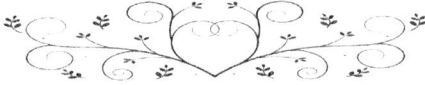

82.

Once we experience oneness — the true nature of reality — as we expand our perspective, petty squabbles become meaningless, minor stresses become insignificant, anxiety over social interactions disappear, because all there is love and compassion for others. The self dissolves, dissipating, becoming that energetic field underlying all things, expanding to the entire universe. When we have this universe-sized perspective, what else possibly matters besides the sheer beauty and awe of this universe, the majesty and magic of life itself?

83.

Everything we do, all the entertainment we consume, trains our mind to be in a particular state. The more time we spend in that state, the more we train our mind to react from that state of mind. If we mindlessly consume negative, fear-stoking entertainment, we will train our mind to be fearful and negative. On the other hand, if we consume positive messages, if we practice kindness and generosity, our mind will become more positive, kind and generous. If we practice love and peace, we will find love and peace.

84.

We have all seen in our lives two people experiencing the exact same unfortunate thing. One person will make the best of it, laugh it off or try to find the positive in it. The other person will lose it, go bananas, bounce off the walls, or turn red with rage. The only difference between the two people was the story they told themselves in their heads about what was happening. One person came from a place of ego and felt like this situation shouldn't be happening to them. The other person came from a place of egolessness and gratitude because they nurtured their gratitude and calm abiding.

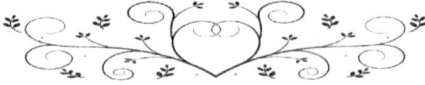

85.

While it's easy to look back at history and see competition as the core of who we are as humans, the correct way to see history is actually through the lens of humans coming together and achieving remarkable things, like the half a million people that it took to put a man into space. Or communities coming together to rescue each other in times of disaster. It doesn't always make the news or the history books, but humans are only here because of cooperation. All the beautiful moments in human history are people coming together, working together, to achieve a greater good.

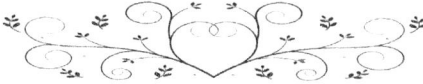

86.

To get out of the competition, we simply have to get out of comparison. As it's been said, comparison is the thief of joy. A house that would make any homeless person exuberant can make another person depressed because they're used to an even bigger house. Most of us are always comparing ourselves and our stuff to people who have even more, but rarely those who have less. This comparative mindset is so profound that there's a greater rate of suicide amongst people who were formerly rich and lost it all, than people who've been homeless or poor their whole lives because once people have gotten attached to something, once they have something better to compare to their lives to, life becomes unbearable.

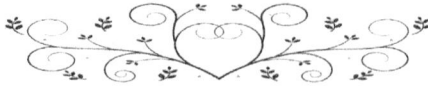

87.

As we search for a life partner, we'll typically date many people, going from partner to partner. But more often than not, we view our love life as going from heartache to heartache. Both are true, it just depends on how we look at our situations. If we see our lives going from rejection to rejection or disappointment to disappointment, we will become jaded and too scarred to have the strength to go on. But if we see the big picture, if we can see the love when it's there and the exciting new opportunities when that love goes away, we can more deeply enjoy our dates' company, and even our solitude when the romance ends. In this way, we won't get so caught up in the ups and downs.

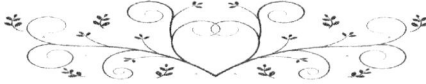

88.

The more peace we have, the more confident and sure we are in ourselves that we don't even need a partner. Then typically, out of nowhere, a partner comes into our lives because you're giving off that energy of confidence and worry-free peacefulness that everyone wants to be around. They suck it up like oxygen. It's intoxicating to be around people who are fully in themselves, fully themselves, and full of inner strength.

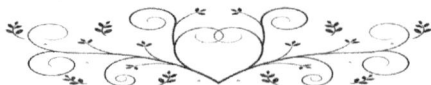

89.

As we bring higher consciousness into our minds, we begin to generate, consciously and with intention, thoughts that serve us, that serve our peace, and create joy. It's like William Shakespeare, the great prophet, once said, "Nothing is either good or bad but thinking makes it so."

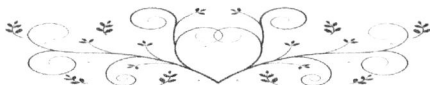

90.

With an expanded perspective, we can value people's different opinions, we can forgive their mistakes, and we can know deep down that everyone is simply doing their best with where they are and what they are capable of in this moment. With an expanded perspective we can see how we can help them with what they're going through, and provide a space for them to be without being judged, criticized or dehumanized. We can simply love, give and forgive.

91.

We all have a tendency to get complacent and repetitive in our daily lives. Over years and decades, that repetition can become a kind of stagnation, almost a mental prison. We get comfortable and over time that comfort becomes unbearable to be without, and yet, hard as we try, things do and will always change. That's why it's important to go a little outside your comfort zone, keep exploring, trying new things, and taking chances. This way, as you get older you'll be able to keep that open-mindedness, that courage, that fearlessness, and that is the key to a big life we can look back on and be proud.

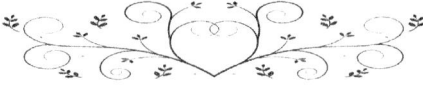

92.

If you're trying to find a dating partner, then if you don't put too much focus on looks, neither will they, and you'll find someone who's a good person and who'll appreciate the good person in you. You will find someone who thinks you're beautiful and it doesn't matter what people who don't see that think and who can't see the real person underneath your skin suit.

93.

When we're disconnected from our spirit and our spirituality, all we see is the physicality of the material world. That's just the superficial stuff, the least important stuff there is. The more you can really go deep and really feel yourself from the inside and experience other people on a much deeper level too, the less the little ups and downs of this very shallow surface world will matter.

94.

If we remember that our life stories are just stories, we will not suffer from them. But because we have these egos that say this or that happened to me, we feel the extra emotional weight from them. If we recall a story from a movie or book, our egos do not suffer.

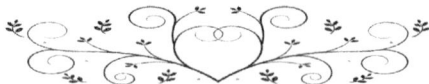

95.

One of the earliest things that happens to almost everybody is they have a moment of this kind of pure bliss, egolessness, and timelessness in meditation. Or, maybe it just comes to them naturally, and immediately their mind says, "That was amazing. I need more of that." And immediately, as the thinking mind starts, you're pulled out of that state. The mind says, "What was that? I want more of that. Let me analyze that for you." But true spirituality is about letting go of everything and realizing you're still whole.

96.

By being fully present we make sure that our mind is not using us, robbing us of this moment, and that we don't reach the end of our lives realizing we missed our whole life because we were always thinking about something else, reliving a past moment, or thinking about the future.

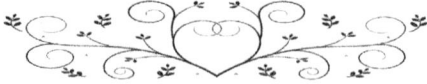

97.

The start of acceptance is really the start of looking closely at what we don't want to see, what we don't like, and have a hard time accepting; because that's the part that needs to be accepted. So look in those dark corners and shine there so brightly with love and self-love until there are no more dark corners left.

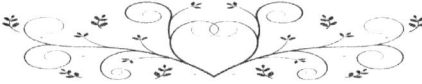

98.

We carry with us so much baggage and so much negativity. We are constantly reliving our worst moments and we're constantly living in the worst imagined future. The truth is that this doesn't help anybody. We can choose what we focus on. We can choose to live in the present moment and focus on all the things that we're grateful for and all the beauty in the world or we can choose to think about the negative things. Ultimately, the choice is ours.

99.

So many times we're focused on something negative happening that we don't even see what's going on around us. Either we're absorbed in the past or in some imagined future that we don't even notice there might be a rainbow right in front of us.

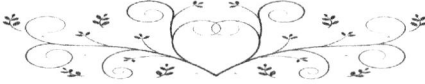

100.

Start observing without labeling and being fully present in the here and now because in the here and now problems don't exist. There may be situations that require our attention, but they in their very nature are not problematic.

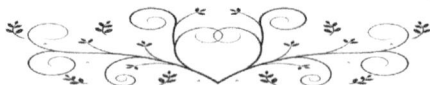

101.

Life will go on experiencing the universe as the universe intended. Everything in the universe is perfect and happening exactly the way it should. It's hard to see that all the time when there's so much suffering in the world, but it tells us that each of us has more to do, has to wake up further, and has more to do towards building a future where everybody can live a fulfilling, safe, and beautiful life.

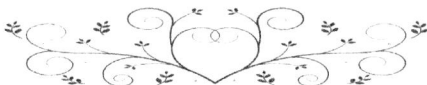

102.

God and the universe are really interchangeable words. The universe loves us, God loves us. Have faith in the universe, have faith in God. It's all the same. If God is everywhere then God is the universe and you don't have to believe in God to believe in the universe.

103.

Most of the time when we start something new, we're not great at it right away. Surprisingly, people who are not great at something right away end up being the best at that thing. This is because the people who have a hard time at first stick with their work, develop discipline and great habits of work ethic, and they constantly improve at their craft. Whereas the person who is a natural ultimately reaches a plateau, as they haven't developed the discipline to stick to it. At the first sign of difficulty, the natural instantly quits. So it's okay if you're not great at your passion when you start. In fact, it's better.

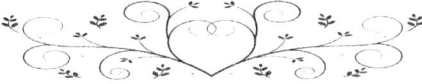

104.

It doesn't matter if we're being judged by a hundred fools or the own thoughts in our head. As long as we know how precious each life is, how precious each moment is, no one's foolish thinking can shake our confidence in that truth.

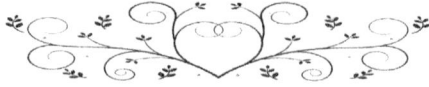

105.

With mindfulness and being able to be present, there is no more reliving or regretting moments from the past. There is only understanding and wisdom gained from these experiences. These are the ways to let go of the past, forgive ourselves, and move forward.

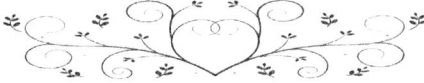

106.

We get attached to certain people and forms and things and situations. But the truth is, things will always change, and by understanding that on a deep level we won't be surprised when it happens to us. We can more easily face loss and surf the now.

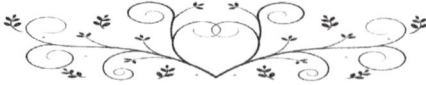

107.

You might be required to take some action now to make your life better in the future. To take those actions, making decisions is necessary. And any indecision based on fear will only lead to more difficulties. Sometimes inaction may be the best course of action, but even that is a decision based on strength and confidence, not indecision which is fear-based and irrational.

108.

All the stress, and all the anxiety, are like waves on top of the ocean. They're just the surface stuff. Beneath that there is a vast infinite ocean of peace and calm, stillness, joy, and bliss. The more we become aware of that, the more those little waves on top of the ocean seem insignificant.

109.

There is no running away from yourself. Some people think, "This city's full of bad people but this other city might be full of good people." Or, "This job is bad, but the next one will be better." No city is full of good people or bad people. No company is full of good people or bad people. Everyone is complex and every one is unique and when you're in an organization or a city with a large number of people, you're gonna have a mixture of both.

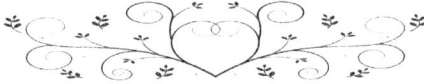

110.

Sometimes when we make a big life decision, whether it's quitting a job or moving cities, we are really trying to run away from ourselves. We hope the next job or the next town will save us. But in reality, we will still find the same problems wherever we go because we can never run away from ourselves.

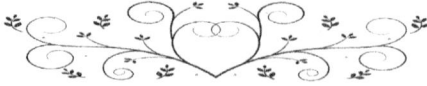

111.

We, humans, are a funny bunch of social creatures. We are not machines who can just change our emotions at will. And one of the things we crave almost as much — if not more so — than food is human connection.

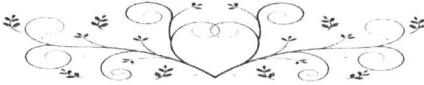

112.

The universe is unfolding in the only way it possibly can, sometimes maybe not as we desire but always in a way we can accept and learn from and grow from.

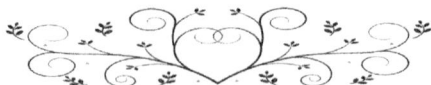

113.

Meditation is not about the time you're sitting down with your eyes closed. It's about how that time impacts the rest of your day and the rest of your life. Meditation isn't just for sitting either. Every single moment of our lives can be a meditation.

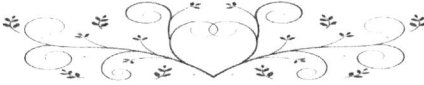

114.

To look into someone's eyes and to have photons firing back and forth between each other, simultaneously connecting to both brains and creating a vision of the other person in one another's mind, this is what happens when we sit with someone. We are taking them into our own minds and our own hearts. There is a merging that takes place. A oneness. It can be felt so greatly and so powerfully as we sit with another person, as we listen to anything they need to say and they to us, or even as we sit in the transforming presence of silent spaciousness.

115.

So much suffering comes because we believe that our thoughts are who we are. So the more we become mindful of our thoughts, the more we can just witness without attachment and identification, making our suffering disappear.

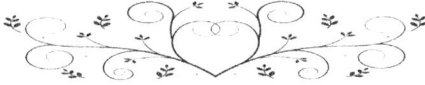

116.

When you feel bored of a city, job, relationship, or any other thing, notice every little thing that's different instead of every little thing that's the same, because every moment is different from the last and there is a beautiful uniqueness in each vibrant moment.

117.

Make a consistent habit of meditation every day at the same exact time and do not miss it no matter what. It doesn't matter if you meditated for 10,000 hours if you haven't done it for 30 years. It needs to be built into a habit.

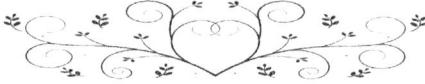

118.

There are many paths to enlightenment. Some of them are service, charity, selfless acts to others, worship and devotion, some are wisdom and understanding, and for some people it's meditation. Very few people stick to just one path, most people follow a combination of these paths. Everybody's different and we have to listen to our minds, our hearts, and our guts.

119.

There are so many things we need to ask ourselves when finding direction, finding purpose, and finding meaning. It's not easy to make these biggest choices in our lives. The only way to find these answers is through meditation, introspection and reflection. We have to give ourselves some space in our lives, to turn off the noise, to tune into ourselves.

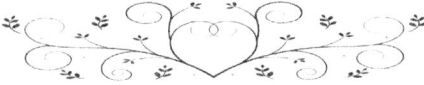

120.

Insecurities are thoughts stemming from anxiety, which stems from fear that we have little or no self-worth in this or that particular area — not good-looking enough, not smart enough, not talented enough, not disciplined enough. Whatever we're currently feeling insecure about is what leads to being self-conscious, having low self-esteem, low confidence, and we become driven by fear rather than fearlessness. All insecurities stem from the perception that there is a "me" made up of this body and this mind, which make up the illusion of who we think we are.

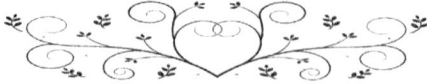

121.

You can't avoid painful memories that you need to deal with and process. You can't stuff them down either. You need to just sit with them and look at them until their presence no longer stirs any agitation. And when agitation does arise, simply bringing your conscious attention to this subconscious process will make the power of these afflictive memories disappear.

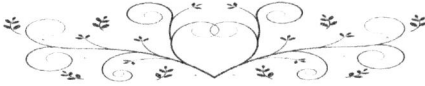

122.

When we have insecurities arise, we have to ask ourselves, "Who are the people we are allowing to judge our self-worth? Are they people who are kind with a good heart and wisdom? Is it our own ego and our thoughts that are criticizing us?"

123.

It's so common to fear the unknown and fear what we don't understand, but that's one of the most important things we can come to accept because it's the only truth there is. When you have full trust and faith in the universe, there's nothing to fear.

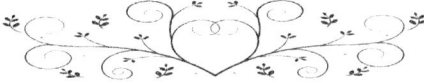

124.

Spirituality is about being fully present, fully alive, fully alert, fully at peace, and in that state of true awe and wonder.

125.

Never forget that every moment is a miracle. That's the goal of spirituality, to never forget that.

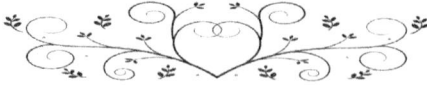

126.

There's so much we miss because we're not fully present. And it may seem mundane, but this is how we add richness to our lives — by becoming aware of everything around us. There is a rich tapestry of experiences always happening around us that we're mostly unaware of and that are waiting to be enjoyed and appreciated by us.

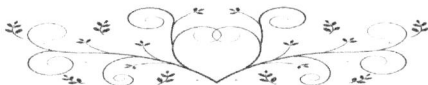

127.

When you remove all the layers of programming that society has created for us — your thoughts, your emotions, your beliefs — what you are left with is your true nature, your true identity, which is your infinite eternal consciousness, your awareness, pure consciousness.

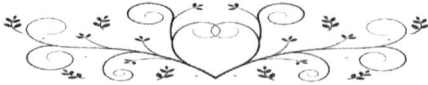

128.

The best thing is to do the things that make us feel self-confident, that get us out of our heads. Most importantly connect with your true selves and realize that we're really not this physical body we're temporarily inhabiting.

129.

Whenever you have a negative thought or a complaint or feeling, all you have to do is just notice it. Don't say, "I don't like this thing." Say to yourself, "This mind is resisting this thing." Because that is a truer statement and that's how we can use the situation as an opportunity to grow in mindfulness. Instantly you will become aware of unconscious thought patterns as you become the witness to the thoughts and not the thinker of your thoughts.

130.

When we expand our perspective, we don't lash out at other people, we recognize they have a life we don't know about. They have an inner life we're even less aware of. We don't know their struggles, we don't know their trauma, and all we know is we would be them if we were in their shoes. We would do what they did because we are all one in different bodies with different experiences, but deep down we all seek love, connection, peace, health and happiness.

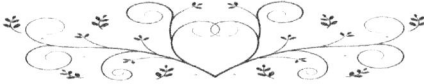

131.

In lower levels of consciousness, we fixate on objects and we compare them to ourselves and our situations. As we meditate, reflect, and expand our consciousness, we notice the relationships between objects and the energy coming from people, animals, plants and everything around us. We feel connected to the sun which gives us life, and the moon for the tides which sustain us. In higher states of consciousness, there's only gratitude and awe. We just have to look deeper to find it.

132.

Part of being present and training our minds to be present through meditation, is about fully accepting this moment, not comparing it to anything from the past or our dreams of the future. It's not about where we feel we should be or what the people we follow on Instagram are doing.

133.

Your heart will tell you which relationships are worth investing in and which ones you need to protect yourself from, because you are worthy of love and generosity and you deserve to find it, share it, and spread it.

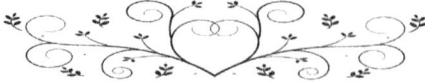

134.

The more we delve into the present moment and let the past be in the past and the future be in the future, the more our ego subsides and a great peacefulness arises. This peacefulness is how we can heal from the past, let go of our worries about the future, and we can go from believing our life story to realizing we are life itself. Only the ego wants to cling to these stories, and presence is how we will let go.

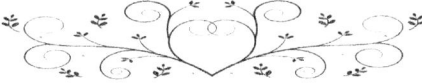

135.

Nobody is perfect, no one has a perfect life. We're all doing our best to live our best lives, and in this process we all make mistakes. So, there's no reason to be harder on ourselves than we would be on anyone else just because we identify with the life we think we possess rather than the life that we actually are.

136.

Being present doesn't mean forgetting about the future. It means being aware of what you're doing in the present, and how it will affect the future in either a negative or a positive way. With this heightened awareness, we can know what to do in the now that will lead to the best possible outcome. So do what you love, live without fear, live courageously, and know that the work you do on your inner growth now will be the greatest investment you can make for your future happiness.

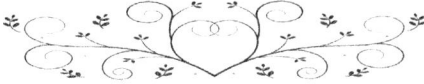

137.

How do we find something to be happy about? The true answer is: to find nothing to be happy about. This is because things can only make us happy temporarily. What we're really looking for is lasting joy, permanent gratitude, endless peace, and eternal bliss. And that can only come from within.

138.

There are times when we are going through a difficult time, and it becomes the hardest to see any good that can come from our suffering. The nature of reality is that struggles help us reach our true potential. There can be no success without failure and there can be no achievement without defeat. These are the stepping stones, the stumbling blocks, on our path to greatness, love, peace and joy.

139.

There will always be ups and downs in our lives. They're unavoidable. But having a strong spiritual foundation gives us a strong presence. Being rooted in presence and gratitude and optimism will armor you up for those low times and they'll make the high times even higher.

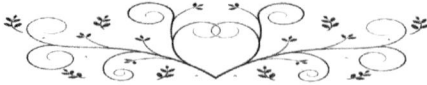

140.

One thing we can do is use meditation for pushing our limits, for achieving that very difficult thing of getting down on that meditation pillow, and we can use it to build up our inner strength in a safe, peaceful, and supportive way.

141.

We're either making good habits or bad habits. We're either training our minds to be unfocused and unhappy, or we're training them to find peace and happiness within.

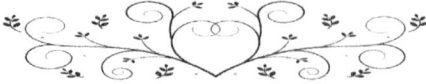

142.

Just as we create stories in our mind of how some painful experience traumatized us, changed us forever, and became a part of our identity; we too can let go of these stories by realizing those moments are gone and that holding onto them doesn't serve us.

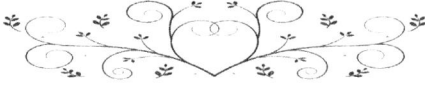

143.

As we become rooted in the present moment, as our inner peace and joy radiate from within us through meditation, we will finally be able to find a mate not out of desperation to be free from loneliness, but rather we'll find someone who, like you, is living life to the fullest and excited to bring a partner on board to share the ride.

144.

When you feel bored of a city, job, relationship, or any other thing, notice every little thing that's different instead of every little thing that's the same, because every moment is different from the last and there is a beautiful uniqueness in each vibrant moment.

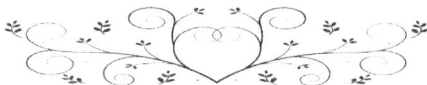

145.

Every single thing about you will change. Your tastes, opinions, thoughts, and preferences will change. Your body will become frail. Your senses may fade. But, the light of consciousness within you will never change, will never flicker, and will never dim. This is the eternal you.

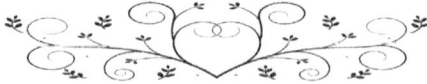

146.

We've all seen the memes about cutting out anyone in your life who drains your energy or doesn't appreciate you. But those people are clearly suffering and maybe we can help them. If we cut every person out of our lives who isn't perfect, we'll have to cut everyone out of our lives, including ourselves.

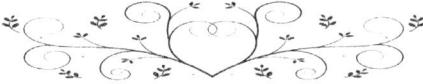

147.

It is in each of our rights to cut off people who are negative and hurtful if done so in a loving and compassionate way. So much talk online these days is about cutting toxic people out of our lives and removing ourself from toxic situations. And while that is very important, it's also important not to go too far that we cut out someone out who tells us a hard truth, to not cut out someone who will tell the truth out of love for us, someone who might make our life inconvenient because we really just want to keep doing negative behavior. And so it's so important to introspect, look inward and meditate on these questions, "Am I cutting someone out too soon? Am I not showing compassion to someone who needs it? Are they mean or are they being honest because they love me?"

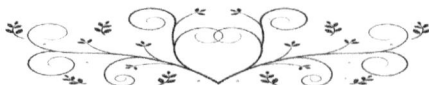

148.

So often, new beginnings can bring with them feelings of failure. Whether we're 40 or even 80 years old, starting something new can feel terrifying. We hear stories of how kids can learn new things easily, but once adults reach a certain age it becomes impossible. Or, we work so hard building a certain life only to realize that once we have it, we actually want something different. Just remember that it's never too late to start again.

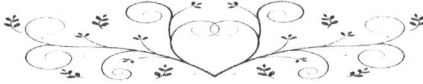

149.

How we treat others is a reflection of how we treat ourselves. When we see others' faults, it's often because we have those same faults. Because our outer world takes place within our mind, how we act toward others is an action toward ourselves.

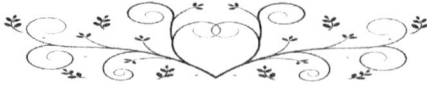

150.

Kindness is not naive or weak. It is strength and a greater understanding that being kind is the only way this world can live in peace and harmony. Niceness can be timid or passive-aggressive, allowing people to take advantage of you, walk all over you, and treat you badly. With kindness, you can firmly say no, without anger or rage, but rather from a place of calm strength that says, "This is unacceptable behavior, I won't stand for it, but I love you and I will allow you the space to learn and evolve." That is kindness. That is how we heal each other and the world.

151.

When we operate from our ego, we have a very small, narrow perspective. Looking at things from a broader perspective, from other people's perspective, or even from the universal perspective, a much greater wisdom can arise within us.

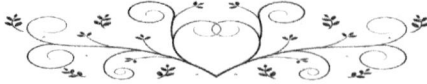

152.

An old buddhist master once told me, "Our minds are like gardens. We either tend to them and give them water, sunshine, and all the things it needs; or we don't and let weeds grow, let the plants and flowers wither away, and we won't get the fruits that we so need. We can't always control our mind and our thoughts right away, but we can plant the seeds of peace and compassion, we can tend to the garden with love, and over time we can bear the fruit of our labor.

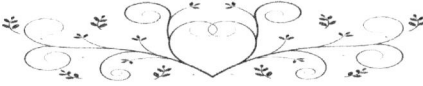

153.

Every thought we have shapes and clouds our view of what is happening all around us. It either sees things as positive, negative or neutral. How it chooses to see different situations depends on how we've been tending to the garden in our mind.

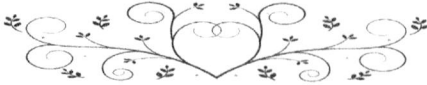

154.

We are born into this world and then quickly told the rules of capitalism: to make as much money as we can. And there's no limit. There's no final number where we can just relax after we reach it. And so, we live our entire lives trying to reach this mountain peak that is never-ending. It's like our human bodies are governed by the laws of physics and our minds are governed by this software program that has set the rules that say you need currency for everything and you need to work for currency, and there will never be enough money. This mindset can turn neighbors into competitors and create a selfish and individualistic culture.

155.

It's so easy and alluring to get caught up in the work we do and the chase for more. In some east Asian countries with high suicide rates, the number one reason is job-related — either losing a job or not getting a job — because their identity becomes entangled with their profession, and their sense of self and honor are derived from this false identity.

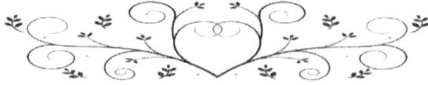

156.

Oftentimes, when making a life change, the greatest difficulty comes from our fear of change. We fear being alone far more than we actually dislike being alone. We allow fear to overpower us and create more resistance and more suffering. In reality, when we're alone, it's just peace. Only our minds stir up unpleasantness. We can easily get so used to having someone around that we forget we can stand being alone. But, we can regain that joy of being with ourselves. It just takes practice and patience. We can remember that one day we'll look back on the time we had alone with fondness. Because the grass is always greener, we can remember to enjoy solitude while we have it.

157.

The good news is, competition is only a made up concept in order to keep us spending and working. It's okay to set goals, have ambitions, and work towards your passions. It's wonderful to be dedicated and committed to achieving your dreams, as long as you don't lose yourself in the proces; as long as you don't lose your joy and purpose in life; as long as you make a life worth living; as long as your job is just a job; and as long as you don't mistake the the journey for the destination, because the journey is what really matters.

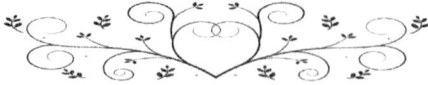

158.

The present moment is so much richer, and more dynamic, and has so much more depth than anything we can think about, any thought about our future, or some memory from the past. The difference is like seeing in 3D and memory is only in 2D.

159.

The truth of the matter is, every single person on earth is a miracle that defied impossible odds to be here today. Every little thing had to go exactly the way it did for the last 14 billion years for each of us to be here today. Just being is a miracle.

160.

No one can predict the future. We can't know what's going to happen and there is no certainty. Sometimes, we worry so much about the future, we miss out on the present. And sometimes, we think we're building a safe and predictable life, and then suddenly the unexpected happens and throws a giant curveball at us. All we can do in such cases is breathe and keep moving forward.

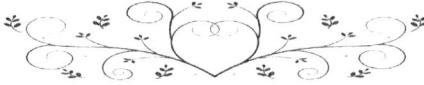

161.

Insecurity is allowing ourselves to criticize ourselves in ways we wouldn't allow for any other person we know to criticize us. Whenever we feel insecurity, whether from someone else or from our own minds, we have to remember that these are criticisms coming from a lower level of consciousness than what we know to be true, which is, each of us is a miracle, a magical being of infinite potential and infinite worth.

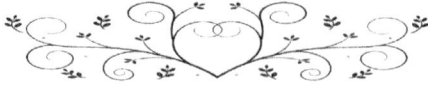

162.

The fact is, for almost everyone out there, someone is better than you at something and someone is worse than you at that same thing. We don't need to measure ourselves against others — especially the greatest of the greats. We just have to do what our hearts inspire us to do with love, joy and passion.

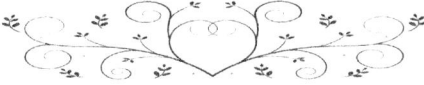

163.

Every decision has its positives and negatives. All you can do is what you think is right and then you have to move forward without looking back. Learn from the past, but move forward without any regret or resentment.

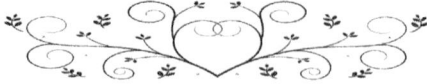

164.

As long as you learn from a mistake, there is no mistake.

165.

Life is all about enjoying the good times while they're here and knowing they won't last. And when the bad times come, we know they won't last either.

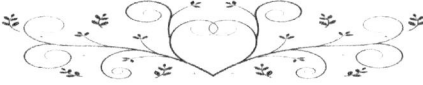

166.

A simple 20-minute, 10-minute, or even five-minute meditation, whatever you're able to do once or twice a day, will create moments of peace and stillness. The more moments of peace you will have in your life, the more that these moments of meditation will spill out into the rest of your day and you will notice like I did, the biggest change in your life that you never thought was possible.

167.

For so many of us, losing a pet can feel more difficult than
losing a person close to us. Unlike people, a pet can be with
you 24 X 7. They'll never push you away, they'll never argue
with you, and so we can develop bonds with pets much more
strongly than even with people sometimes.

168.

Each and every one of us is a mystical healer. We each can be this for one another. It can be as simple as a warm hug that is completely selfless, and you transfer your energy to that person, and you're saying with your body and energy, "I am here for you." This is the greatest act of love there is.

169.

Every little moment of peace that we feel by being present is like a rock in the ocean that leaves ripples going in all directions because these little moments are so precious and so profound that the more we can feel them in our lives, the better.

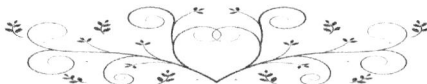

170.

Some people think meditation is a passive state where you're just resting, but in fact, you're at a heightened level of focus, heightened level of attention, heightened level of awareness, and this state is a truly zen state of bliss.

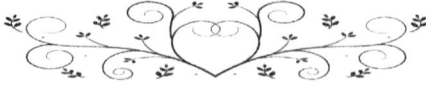

171.

Being present means paying more attention to what you're seeing, noticing how the light changes in the way it reflects off objects throughout the day, notice the way every little thing feels in your fingertips.

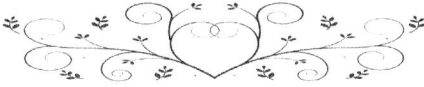

172.

Living in the past or worrying about the future - this is where the ego lives.

173.

Don't be too hard on yourself. Also, don't be too easy on yourself. Take that middle path.

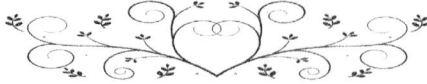

174.

Mindfulness is really about becoming aware of awareness itself and when we do this we identify more with the observer inside us and we identify less with the thoughts in our head.

175.

Mindfulness meditation is like putting on the scuba gear and diving deep, tapping into the deep rich sense of peace and bliss that lies when we are just fully present, fully aware, and fully alert.

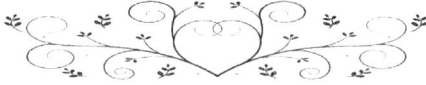

176.

We're so used to having expectations in every aspect of our lives. We put these expectations on ourselves, we're very hard on ourselves, we expect perfection from ourselves and we want to measure achievements and goals and track our progress. But in meditation, we put all that aside and focus on just being.

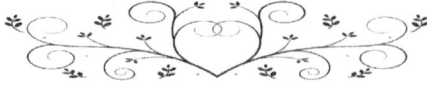

177.

Fear is an insidious little monster. It's a train of thoughts that doesn't announce itself as fear. It pretends to be rational and cautious, but in excess, it's a cancer that diminishes our life's potential. It won't scream "I'm fear," but it will weigh on your shoulders as doubt, insecurity, excess consumption, stress and dis-ease. So, instead of running away from fear, let's turn, look and face fear so that we can recognize it for what it is and let it go.

178.

Losing a pet is one of the most painful experiences we can go through. Our little friends become part of the family. And these little buddies are there for us no matter what. They don't criticize us or judge us. They simply teach us what true, unconditional love looks like.

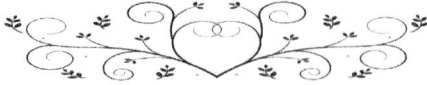

179.

There is always more to a story. Even when you watch a movie something happened before and after what you saw.

180.

Time was not born, time will never die. Things will only change forms.

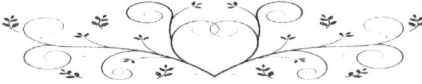

181.

Believe in yourself and ignore the naysayers. This belief in yourself, and the belief that this is your God/Universe-given purpose, these two things alone will sustain you. It is not uncommon for super successful people to believe that success was in their destiny. Don't be afraid to have this crazy amount of confidence and belief in yourself. If anyone can achieve their dreams, you can too.

182.

When we are present in the moment, there is no self-doubt, there are no negative emotions, there is just being in the world, flowing through whatever comes our way, not resisting or fighting, and it is just a joy. In this joy, in this trial and error of life, wherever you are, just keep moving forward. Soon, a confidence will emerge so strongly that no matter what comes your way, you'll be able to handle it with grace and strength. You'll know deep down that in this life, everything won't always go the way you wished, but that you will be able to handle whatever comes your way, turning negatives into positives and challenges into opportunities.

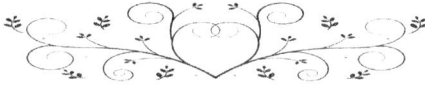

183.

We have to look at our lives without distraction and observe the things we naturally gravitate towards — the things that really get our hearts jumping. We have to always be open to opportunities — seeking them out and creating them. When we act most within our nature is when we are at our happiest.

184.

Life doesn't come with a guidebook. We're not given a crystal ball. There's no instruction manual. At times, we can feel like a bouncy ball, aimlessly wandering through life. Other times, we can feel like the masters of our destiny. Often, just when we feel like we're in total control, life finds a way to humble us. The only constant is change. We can only to do our best, roll with the punches, not cling to fortunes nor resist misfortunes, and simply enjoy each moment of this beautiful dramedy that is our life.

185.

Finding a passion that helps others will always be in demand. So ask yourself, what is the greatest contribution you can give to this earth? What are you passionate about that brings joy and improves the lives of others? If you have passion and self-belief, which are just states of mind, then you can do anything. In fact, having these two things is the only way anything truly great gets done.

186.

Once you become aware of all the tactics your mind is using to sabotage your peace and happiness, you can use your conscious mind to reframe your opinions, create new more positive beliefs, and create a new you.

187.

When we do an act of kindness when nobody's looking, and without even telling anyone, that is complete selflessness, egolessness, and it sets a good example for the world. The path to liberation is paved in selfless service. Be an example by always being kind.

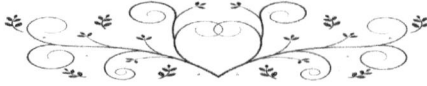

188.

As we bring conscious awareness to our thoughts, the incessant negative thinking stops, because only unconsciously would we ever think negative thoughts that create suffering.

189.

The first step to changing our likes and dislikes starts with becoming aware of the fact that you can choose them.

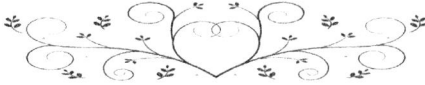

190.

You may carry your suffering with you, but it's a small part of you. However, the ego wants to make it as big as possible because that feeds the ego. It feeds the thinking.

191.

It doesn't matter where you came from or what you've done. Every moment is an explosion of potential and possibility.

192.

We don't actually suffer because things don't go our way. We suffer because we expect things to always go our way.

193.

Lasting joy comes when we make total peace with ourselves, our thoughts, and our situations.

194.

The biggest source of distress in our lives comes from an inability to let go of the past, to be present, to set down that baggage, and to move forward. Our second greatest source of disturbing emotion is an untruthful, unfair, and harsh opinion of ourselves.

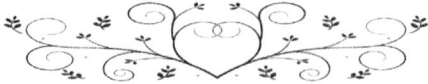

195.

We're bombarded with hundreds of thousands of images every single day from advertising to social media to magazines telling us what is beauty, telling us that whatever we look like is not good enough and we need their products. So, let's not create some kind of artificial standard of beauty as our goal because it really just doesn't matter.

196.

Solitude is nothing to fear and it shouldn't be a motivating factor to find love because if it is, it will set the relationship up to be a co-dependent relationship.

197.

Relationships are about two complete people coming together and being one, not about two half-people who have holes in them and are only looking for somebody to fill them up.

198.

Anxiety can often make us closed off to the world. Taking risks and putting yourself out there can become an insurmountable obstacle. Letting go of our anxiety doesn't just improve our life. It improves the lives of those around us as well.

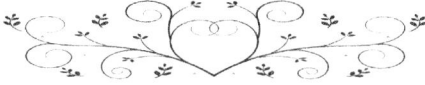

199.

In trying to maintain rocky relationships, remember that every single one of us has gone through some experience, no matter how big or small, that has shaped us in some way or another. When someone acts out, the acting out is not the whole picture. We must remember that every action has a cause, and understanding this is where compassion comes from.

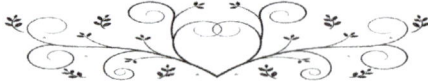

200.

Connection is healing. People who live in close communities heal faster. This is why ancient kings would banish people from their kingdoms to live alone forever as a punishment worse than death.

201.

Life's too short to half-live it, to limit ourselves. We can follow our passions, we can change careers, we can change our old habits and our old ways of thinking.

202.

Neither our pain nor our joys define us. We are consciousness itself having a beautiful experience, always learning, always seeing new and different experiences that give us wisdom and understanding.

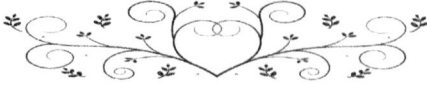

203.

There are no wrong decisions in life, except for indecision.

204.

With every wrong decision comes an incredible learning opportunity that can be so invaluable to our growth.

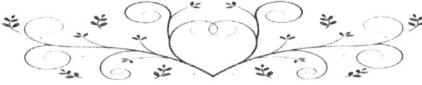

205.

There can be no success without difficulty because otherwise everyone would be equally successful and it wouldn't be called success. There must be the challenge, the discipline, and the fortitude that is only developed and forged in fire.

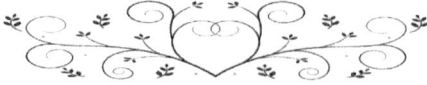

206.

There are no rules set for us except for the ones we set for ourselves. There are no limits except the ones we imagine and believe. As long as there is breath in your body and life in your eyes, you can find new love, you can pursue new passions, can grow and evolve and change any way you wish. All you have to do is take one courageous leap into the present moment and realize that this is where you are, see where you want to go, and begin the path to get there.

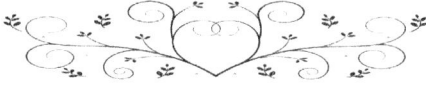

207.

People who have the courage to start over possess bravery far greater than anyone else, because the only reason we don't start over or try something new is because of fear — fear of failure and fear of the unknown.

208.

It doesn't matter if a smile is returned, you still smiled. Smiles are free and you have an infinite supply of them. Give them away to everyone and the people who smile back — you'll know they are your people.

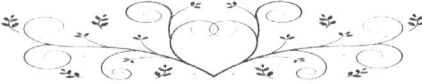

209.

In order to free ourselves from insecurity, we must first develop a deep understanding of what insecurity is, where it stems from, and how it spreads its little seeds of doubt and fear. Once we understand the nature of our own insecurity, we can recognize it for what it is. Once we recognize it, it can no longer hold its grip on us. Once it no longer grips us, we can finally become free from it.

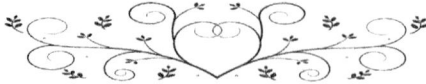

210.

We are magic and I use that term in the sense that it is inexplicable by science why there is life, how it started, why there is something instead of nothing, and how we are all here today walking and talking inside these mysterious bodies.

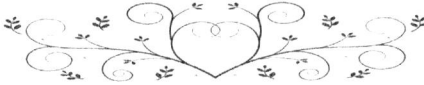

211.

There is a secret to the universe which I have discovered in my life and have observed in others: the bigger your ambitions are to help others, the more the universe will conspire to help you achieve them. So, the bigger the dream, the better.

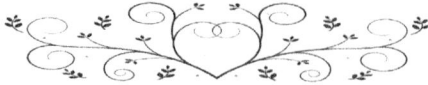

212.

The greatest gift we can give anyone is not jewelry or flowers or a new MacBook pro. It is to simply give our attention to someone — our full, complete, 100% attention. This is to allow someone else to become a part of you, to allow their space to be, without judgment or labels, with total acceptance. This is what true healing is all about.

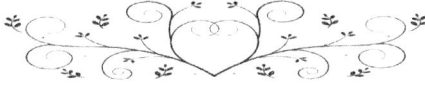

213.

Just by the simple act of sharing space, putting a hand on someone else's hand, embracing in a hug, and allowing your two hearts to get within an inch of each other, two hearts beating in unison, and to breathe in the same pattern as naturally happens, we can give love and healing.

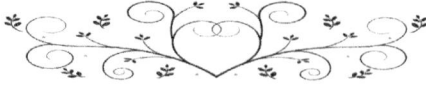

214.

When we lose a pet, so often they're in great pain and it's beautiful to remember their body is doing its natural process to put an end to that pain.

215.

If there was no love, there'd be no grief.

216.

Many people hate every job they've ever had, even their fantastic dream jobs. Similarly, many people hate every city they lived in. And they move and they move and they keep thinking the next one will be the one that ends all their problems, but they don't realize that they are trying to run away from themselves. Wherever they'll go, they'll bring their problems. They'll bring their mindset, they'll bring their coping mechanisms, and they'll bring their addictions.

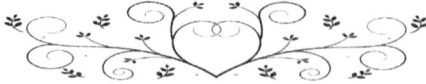

217.

Fear is a pattern that we develop over years and that impacts everything we do in a negative way. It can lead to paralysis in choosing big decisions or avoiding situations that can help us grow. So face your fear, go through it and transform it into your strength.

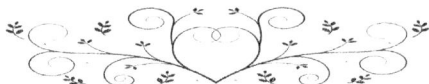

218.

Make every activity in your life a meditation practice by being fully present in whatever you're doing because that's what meditation is.

219.

While meditating, we focus on our breath because it's only happening in the present moment; it is our doorway to the present moment.

220.

To experience every situation as new and miraculous, you have to focus on your senses instead of focusing on the sense objects.

221.

Anything real is more profound than an imagined version of it, so the more we get out of our heads and the more we get into the present moment, and the richer our lives become.

222.

When you don't put the weight of the past on to the present moment, then every moment can feel brand new and incredible.

223.

The heightened awareness that comes from mindfulness can really increase our enjoyment of everything.

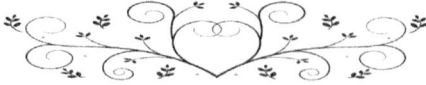

224.

Do not despair over your struggles, for you are blessed with the strength to lift others up.

225.

As we let go of the past and we even let go of our expectations for the future, we can see and heal from our suffering, and we can turn our attention to the here and now.

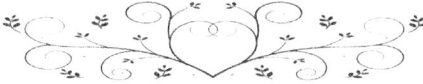

226.

Neither our pain nor our joys define us. We are consciousness itself having a beautiful experience, always learning, always seeing new and different experiences that give us wisdom and understanding.

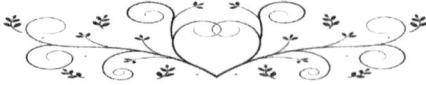

227.

The more you allow your mind to be present without being bombarded with thoughts, opinions, and judgments, the more peace and spaciousness you're going to feel in your life.

228.

To truly change the way we approach love, we have to go to the source of everything we do: our minds.

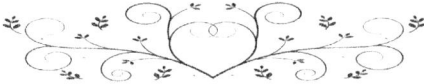

229.

The sooner you can remember to bring your conscious awareness to your anxious thoughts and feelings, the sooner they can be released. Through practice and over time you'll be able to recognize anxiety even before it arises.

230.

Solitude is a gift in itself, it is our blank canvas to paint our lives. It is a beautiful sacred time, full of infinite possibilities - only limited by your imagination.

231.

What matters the most is how good a person is, not how good their follower count is. So, the best thing you can do is to nourish your own inner kindness and compassion.

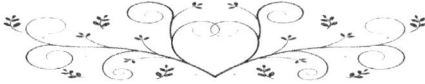

232.

Too often, people act out from a place of hurt and pain. These people are not toxic and they aren't traumatizing. They've been traumatized. So it's more important than ever — as society becomes more fragmented, fractured and isolated — to create strong bonds with people who we can truly be ourselves with, who we can be compassionately honest with. Those are the people and relationships worth fighting for.

233.

If we feel love towards someone else, we feel love. If we feel love towards ourselves, we feel love. This is why being kind to others is being kind to yourself.

234.

If we expand our perspective, if we can feel the interconnectedness of all things and all beings, we will notice the beauty that each act of kindness brings to the world

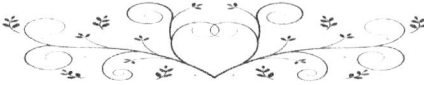

235.

Kindness can be confrontational, but with compassion, love and support. When we express this kind of kindness, there is no ego that gets hurt in the other person because they can tell immediately that we are coming from a place of love.

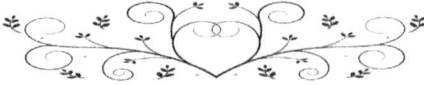

236.

It is a miracle that the infinite number of things that had to happen for me to be here talking to you and you to be there listening were able to happen in just the right way. We are but tiny specks living on a tiny speck of rock, in a tiny galaxy in an infinite universe. Like ants on an anthill building their cities, living their lives, doing what is important to them at the moment, without falling for the trick that they are the center of the universe.

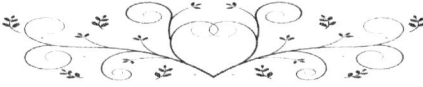

237.

Life is not a winner-take-all game. Human history is not a series of competitions and wars. The truth is, history is a series of human beings coming together to achieve extraordinary things. We are stronger together than we are alone. We need each other and we thrive together.

238.

While the world may seem cruel and competitive, coming together to support one another, to lift up one another, is how we will create a new world. We cannot change the world alone — although change does start within. But to truly create a world we wish to live in and one we wish to leave for the future, we must build it together and for each other. This is the way of peace, harmony, and coexistence.

239.

All you have to do is take one breath at a time, take one step at a time, and take one day at a time. You don't need to carry your entire future on your shoulders — just this moment because that's all there is.

240.

We must see beyond our perspectives, beyond borders and cultures, beyond nations and races, and see the light of consciousness in others as the same within ourselves.

241.

Every single human on earth will one day become old and, by modern standards at least, ugly. This is a crazy modern concept in which we say age is not beautiful. But it is beautiful, and hopefully, it's coming for you too. If we're lucky, it's coming for us all and everyone's going to be in the same boat. So the best thing we can do is build a beautiful life with beautiful people on the inside, tune out the noise and tune into your spirit, your soul, your animating energy that makes you who you are because that's what matters.

242.

Our life story can only define us if we define ourselves by this story.

243.

Letting go of your ego-driven desire to achieve some state or enlightenment is the first step to reaching that state of pure being.

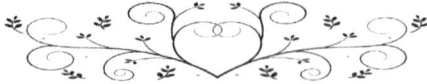

244.

Let go of everything you're holding on to. Let go of all concepts and your sense of identity, the thoughts of how you feel about every little thing, and just be. Just experience and identify with the one who is aware of the experience. Everything we experience can only exist because of our conscious awareness. Nothing happens without it.

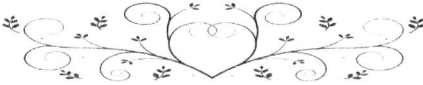

245.

The true source of our life is our consciousness and awareness, without which we'd just be a robot or a computer with no operator.

246.

When you can become aware of awareness, that's the higher consciousness and it's within you. So, instead of looking to the universe for a sign, look inward.

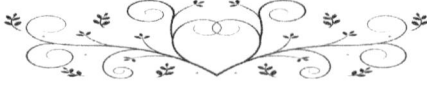

247.

As we breathe the air from the trees, we become the trees. As we eat the food of the earth, we become the food of the earth. We realize that we are all one — interconnected. As we expand our perspective, loneliness disappears, rivalries dissolve, and only love remains because loving all is loving ourself.

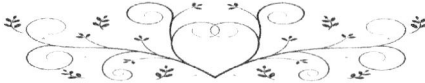

248.

The number one rule of meditation is to get rid of expectations. Toss them out the door as you don't need them.

249.

You are consciousness itself having a perceptual experience. You are consciousness able to perceive and act upon this world.

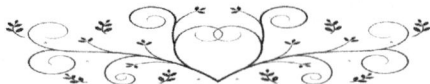

250.

You are this moment.

ABOUT THE AUTHOR

Todd Perelmuter is a spiritual philosopher and renowned speaker on the nature of the human mind. He has impacted the lives of millions worldwide through his teachings in the award-winning spiritual documentary, Aloneness to Oneness.

Todd's goal is to make sure everyone has the tools to realize their full potential, become their most enlightened selves, and make this world a happier and more peaceful place. He shares his timeless wisdom on Youtube and on the Path to Peace with Todd Perelmuter podcast, helping millions realize they are bigger than their thoughts, more than their past, and with limitless potential for living a life beyond their wildest dreams.

Having seen so many people around him suffering from stress, addiction, suicide, anxiety and depression, he decided to leave his comfortable life in New York City as a highly awarded writer and creative director at the world's largest ad agency. Having given away all of his belongings, he left his luxury high-rise apartment in New York and embarked upon a 9-year journey that would take him to over 35 countries across five continents living with shamans, gurus, monks, and tribes. He studied 16 religions and spiritualities, studied with leading researchers in cognitive science, and spent over a year meditating in total solitude, all in an effort to discover the secrets to a peaceful mind.

Todd's teachings have liberated thousands of people from their years of suffering through his work at the non-profit EastWesticism, an organization dedicated to bringing ancient wisdom and modern science from around the world to people everywhere. Go to EastWesticism.org to learn more and see how you can join in this important cause.

Perels of Wisdom

Printed in Great Britain
by Amazon